DOT TO DOT
CAFE SCENES
FOR ADULTS

This book includes 30 Unique Dot Pages.

Start from 1st Number dot and continue all the way till you reach end of numbers, all the designs are continous lines and there are no jumps or breaks!

If you have any suggestions or ideas, please drop an email to
info@coloringbooks101.com

Copyright © 2021 by Sonia Rai

TABLE OF CONTENTS

Cafe Scene 1 (917 dots) - Black

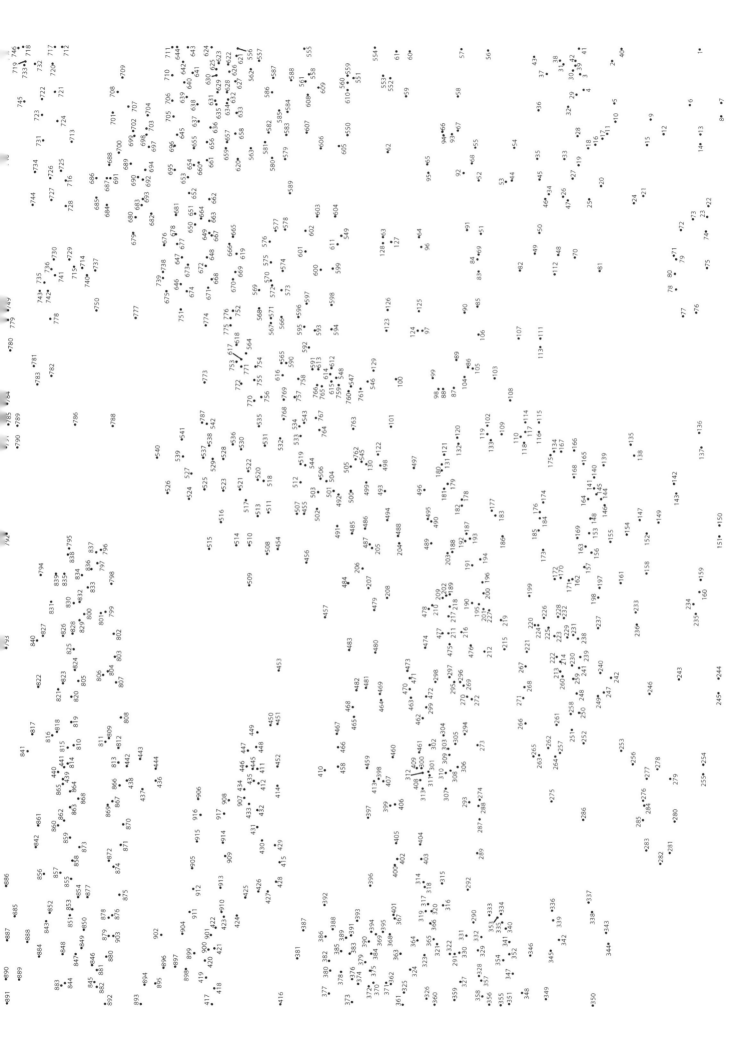

Cafe Scene 2 (938 dots) - Black

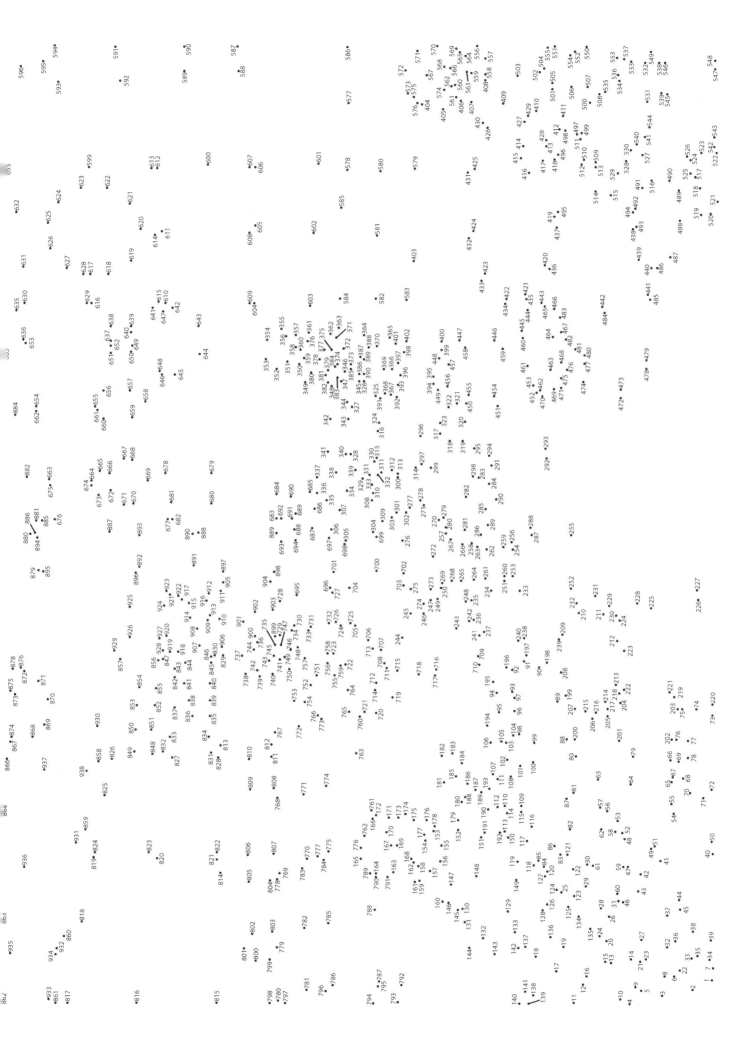

Cafe Scene 3 (1001 dots) - Black

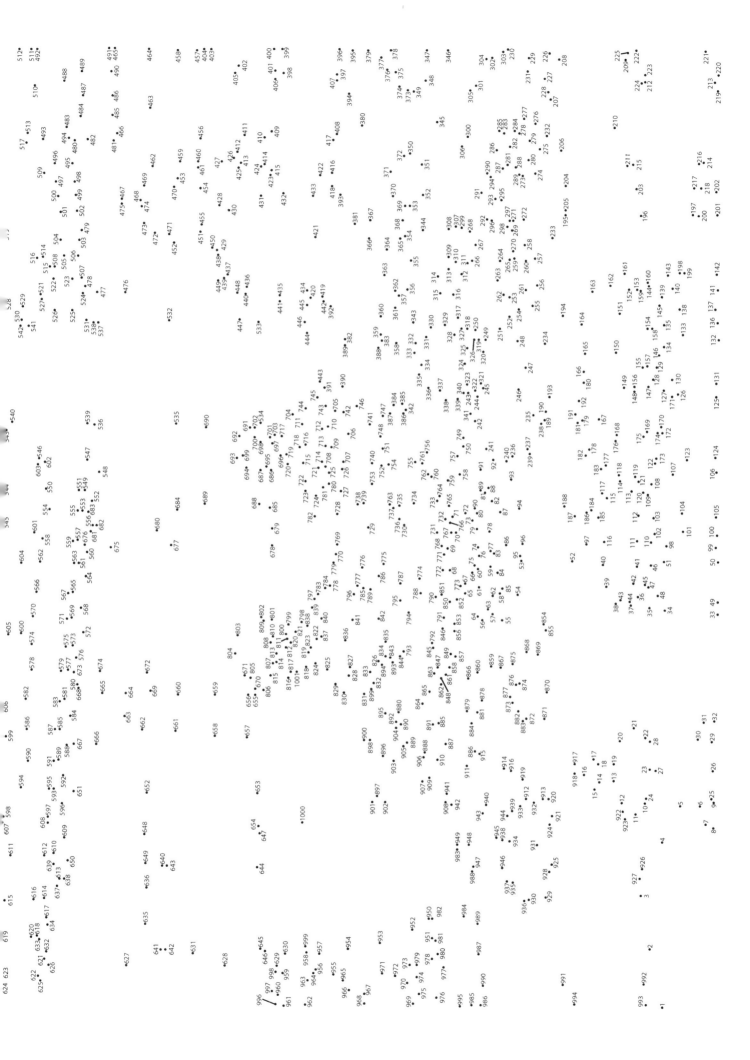

Cafe Scene 4 (745 dots) - Black

Cafe Scene 5 (970 dots) - Black

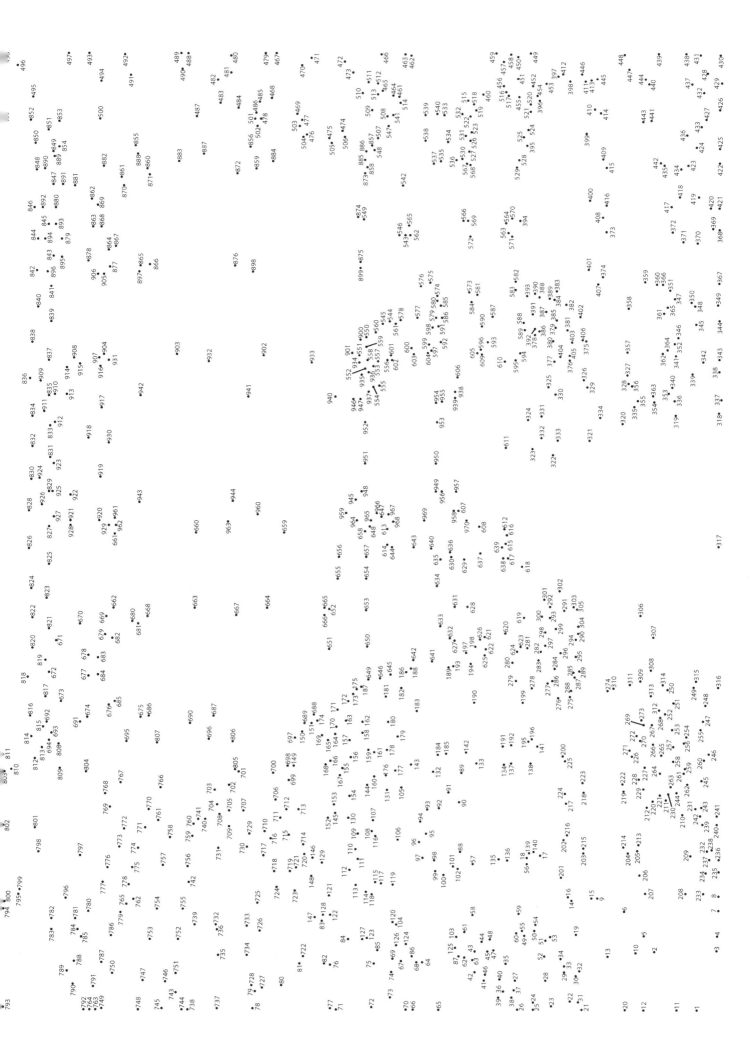

Cafe Scene 6 (903 dots) - Black

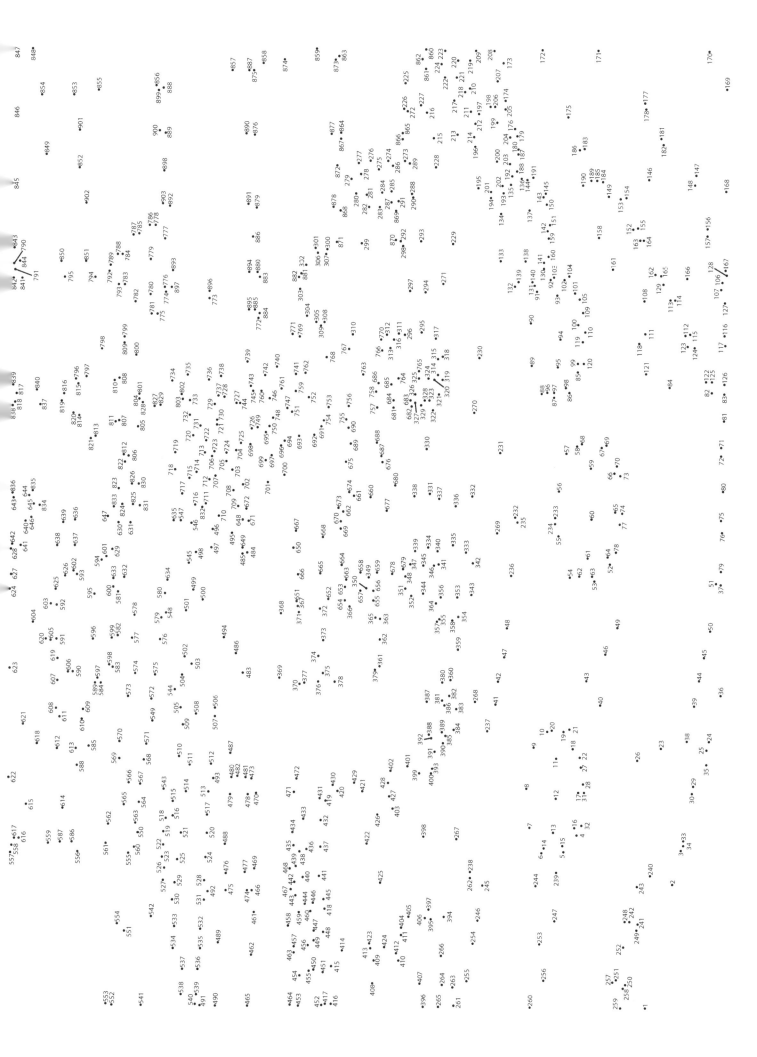

Cafe Scene 7 (900 dots) - Black

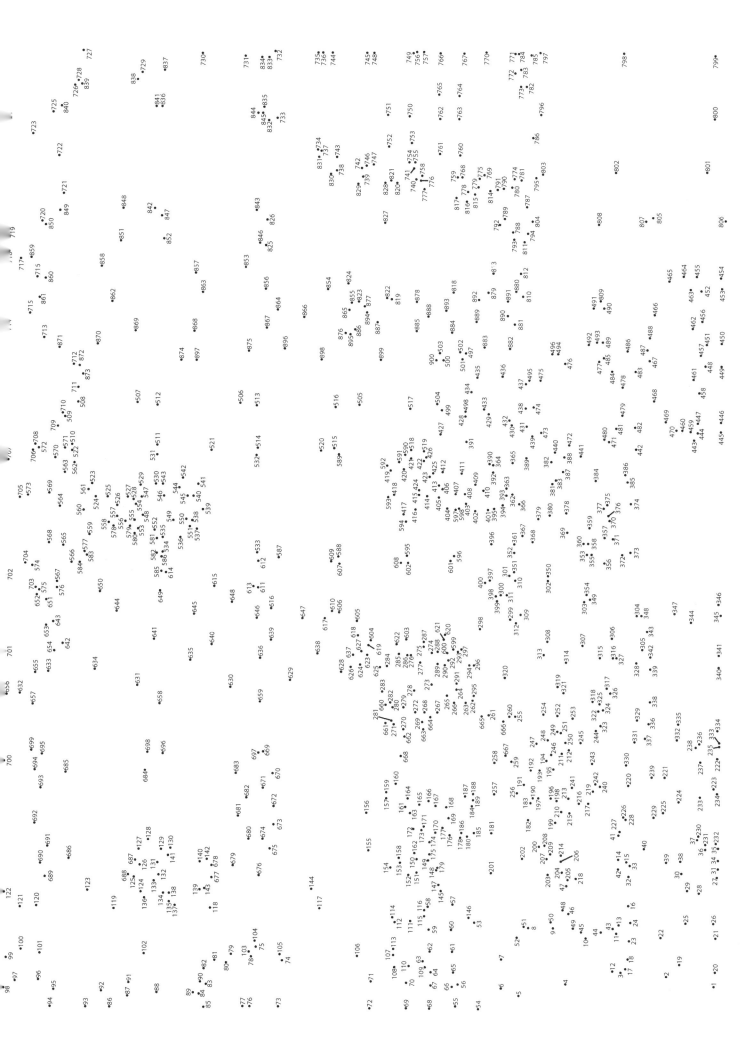

Cafe Scene 8 (705 dots) - Black

Cafe Scene 9 (675 dots) - Black

Cafe Scene 10 (779 dots) - Black

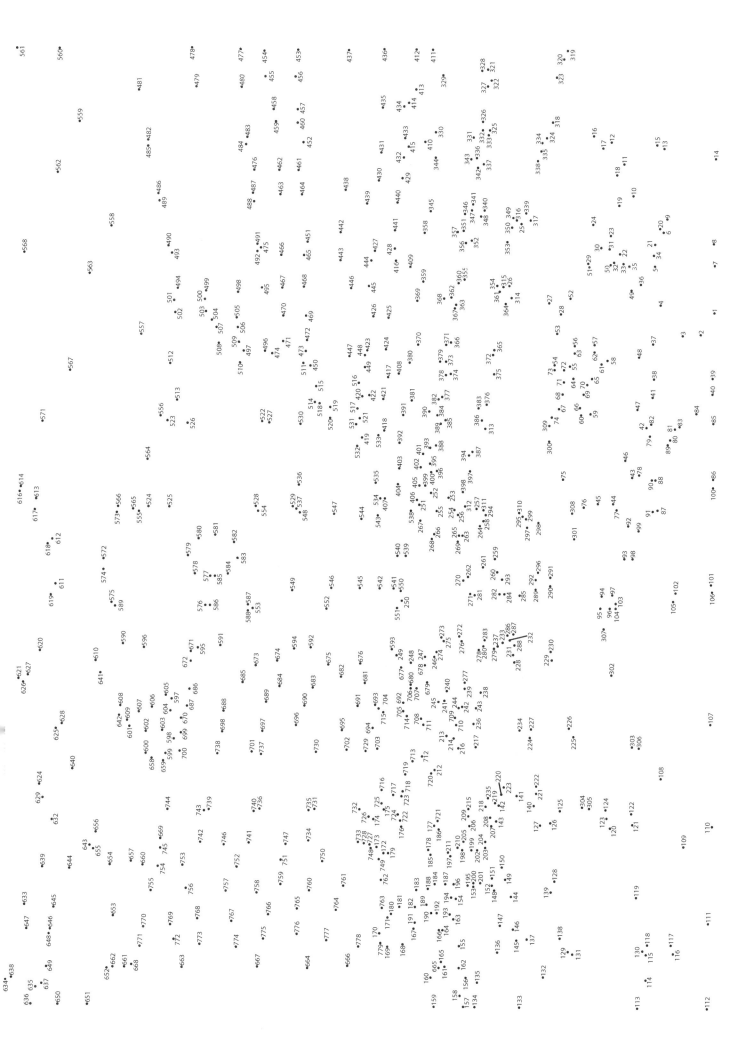

Cafe Scene 11 (805 dots) - Black

Cafe Scene 12 (804 dots) - Black

Cafe Scene 13 (831 dots) - Black

Cafe Scene 14 (772 dots) - Black

Cafe Scene 15 (784 dots) - Black

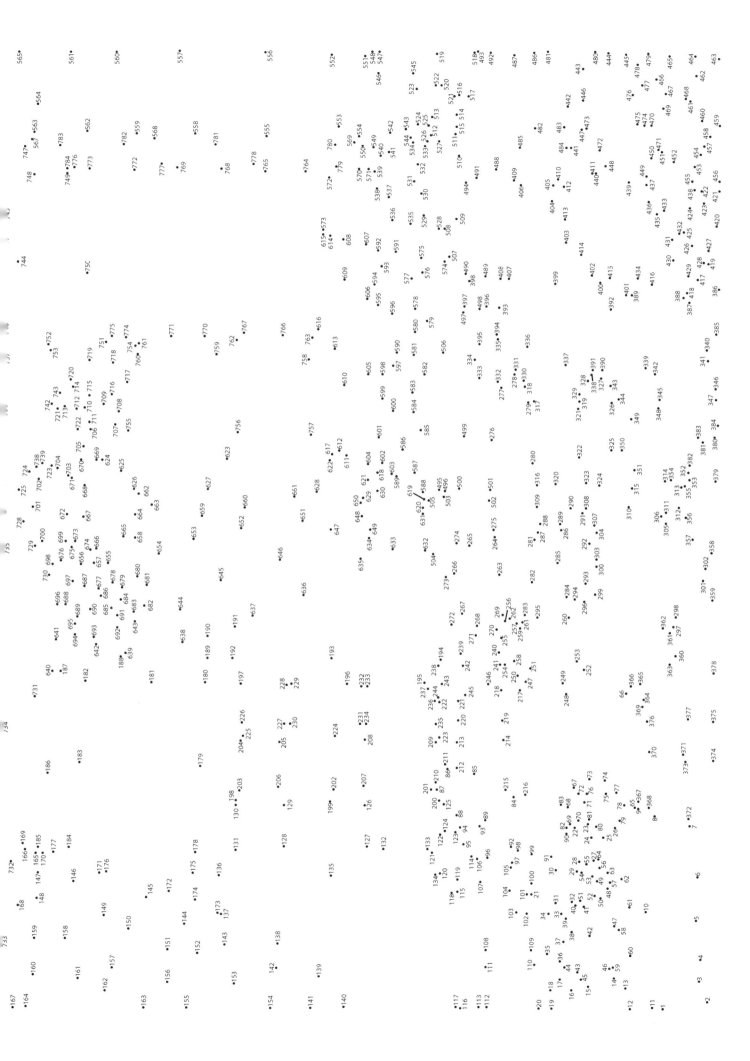

Cafe Scene 16 (920 dots) - Black

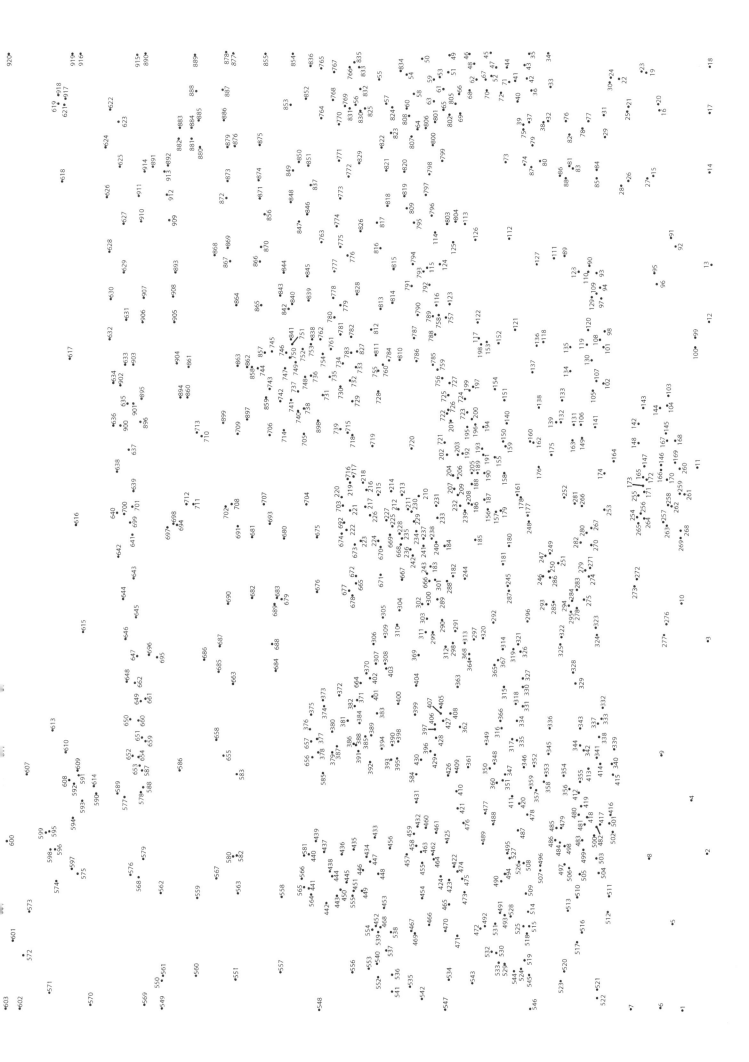

Cafe Scene 17 (913 dots) - Black

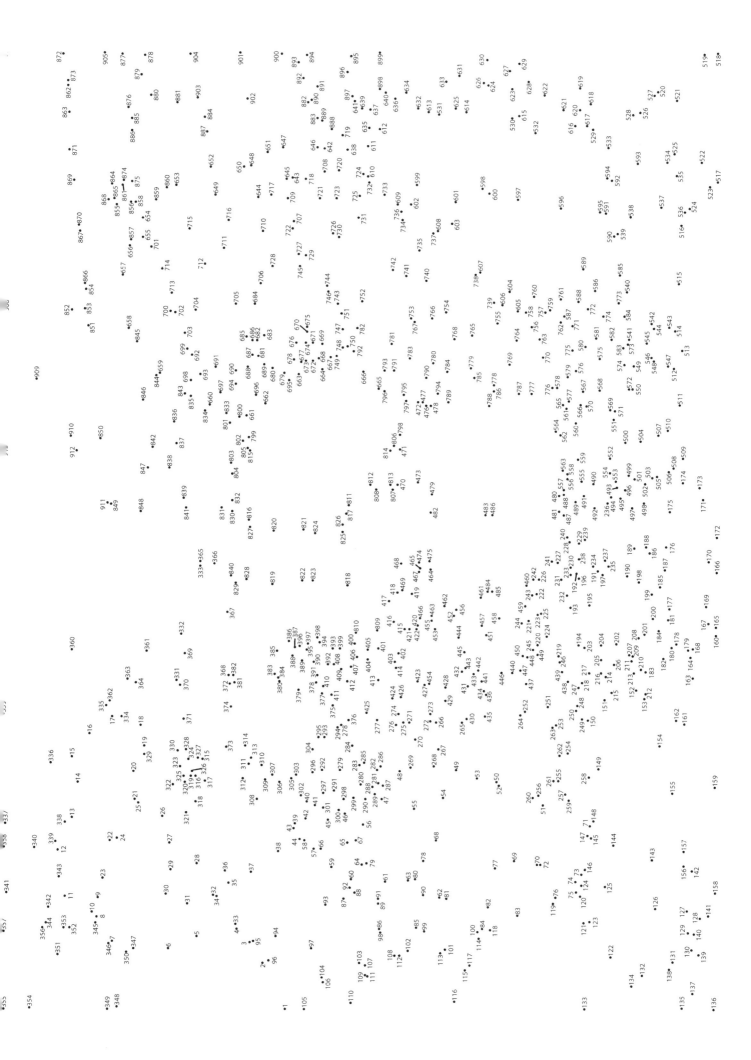

Cafe Scene 18 (718 dots) - Black

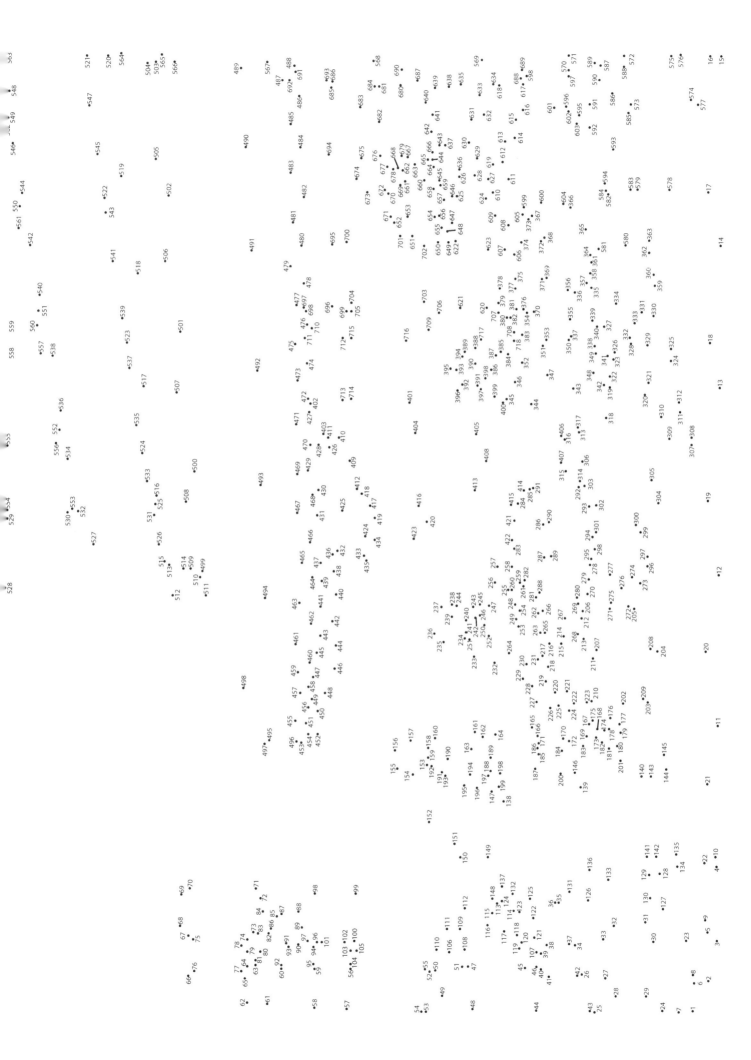

Cafe Scene 19 (815 dots) - Black

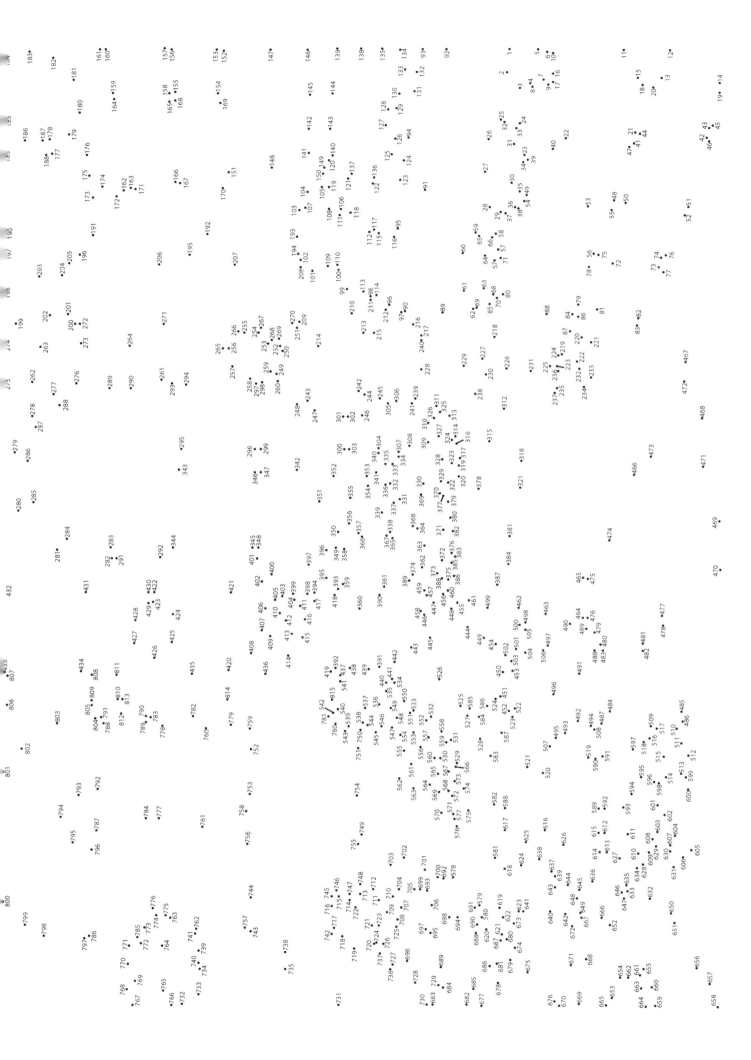

Cafe Scene 20 (916 dots) - Black

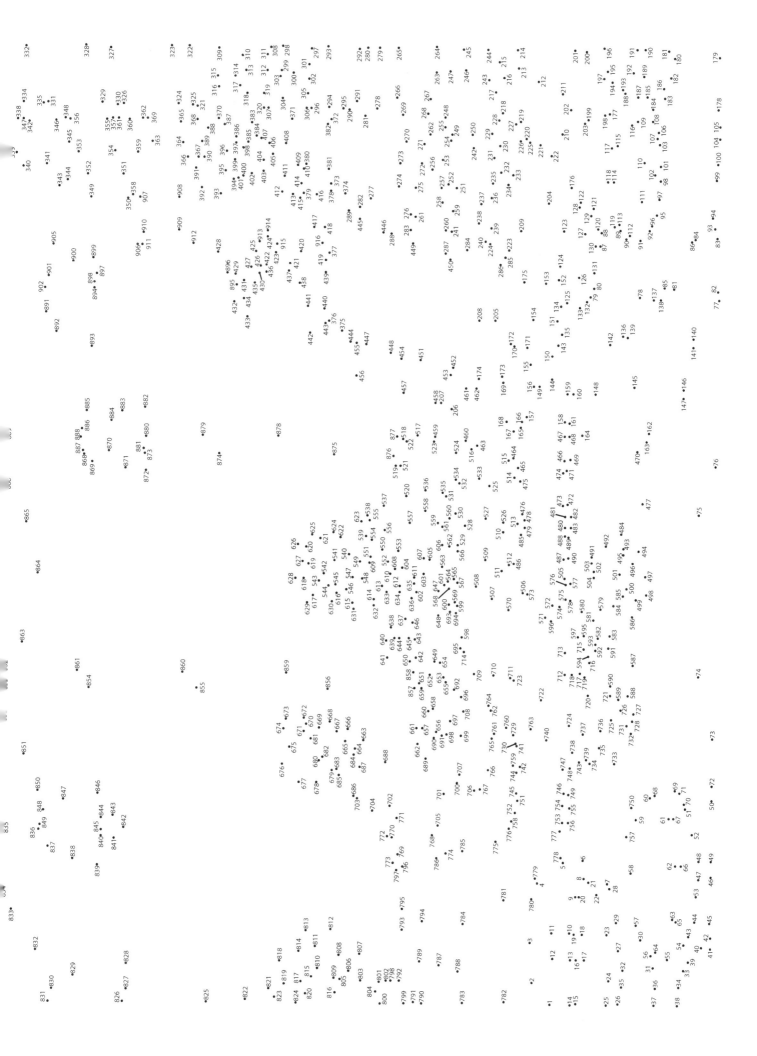

Cafe Scene 21 (897 dots) - Black

Cafe Scene 22 (796 dots) - Black

Cafe Scene 23 (994 dots) - Black

Cafe Scene 24 (704 dots) - Black

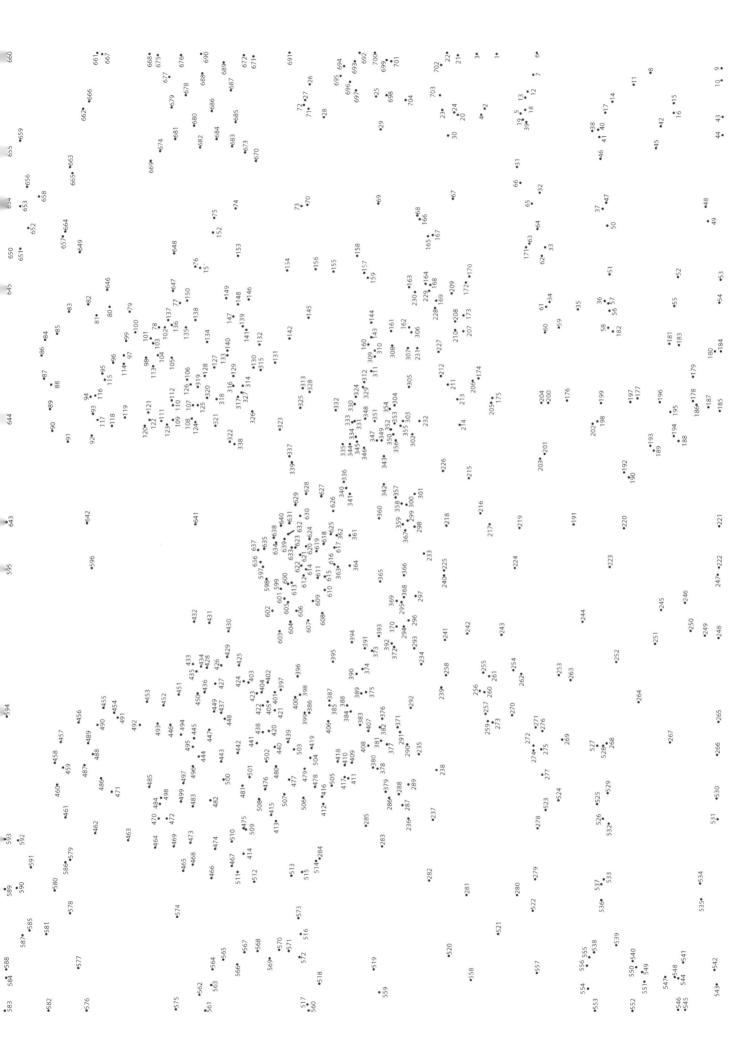

Cafe Scene 25 (785 dots) - Black

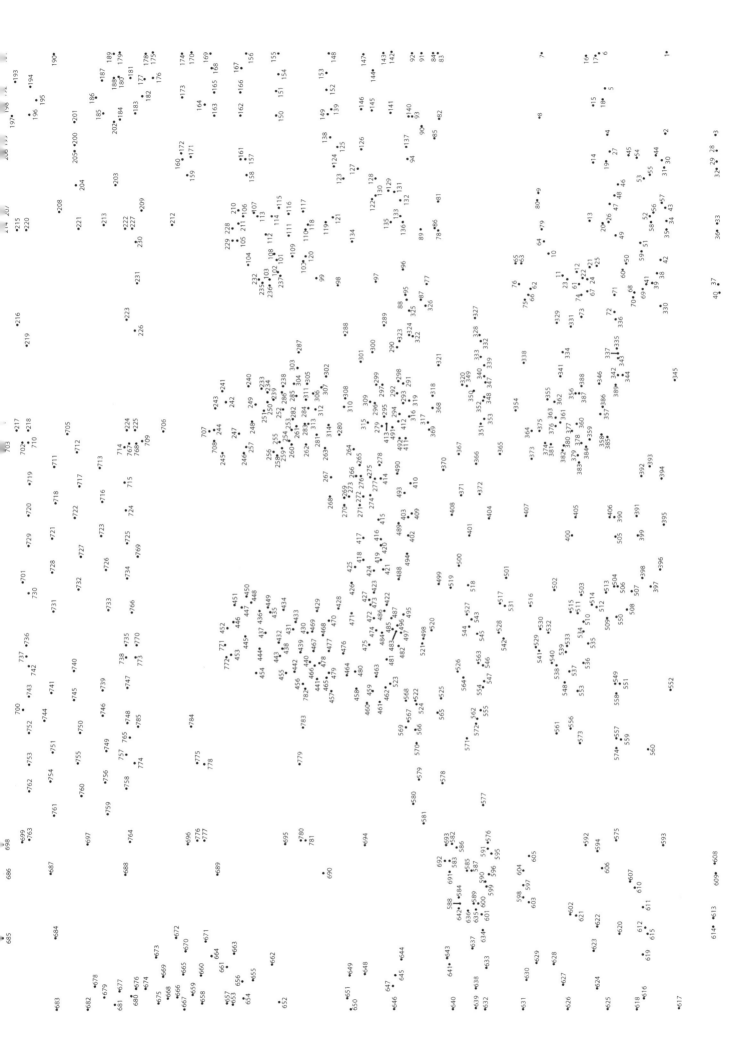

Cafe Scene 26 (753 dots) - Black

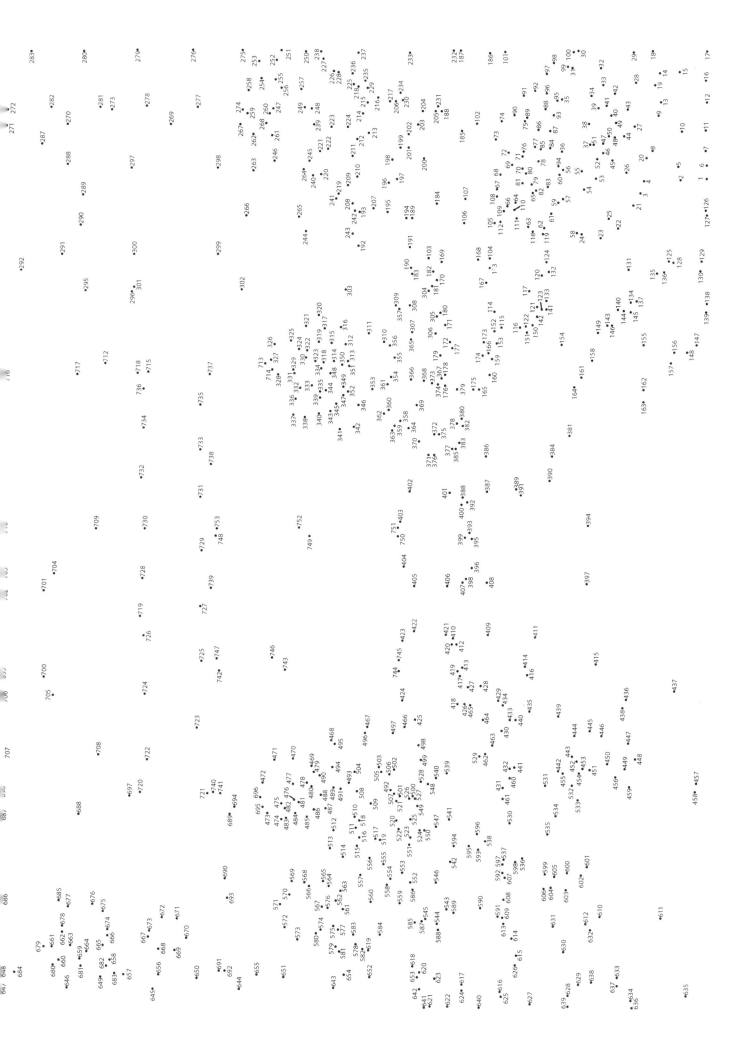

Cafe Scene 27 (851 dots) - Black

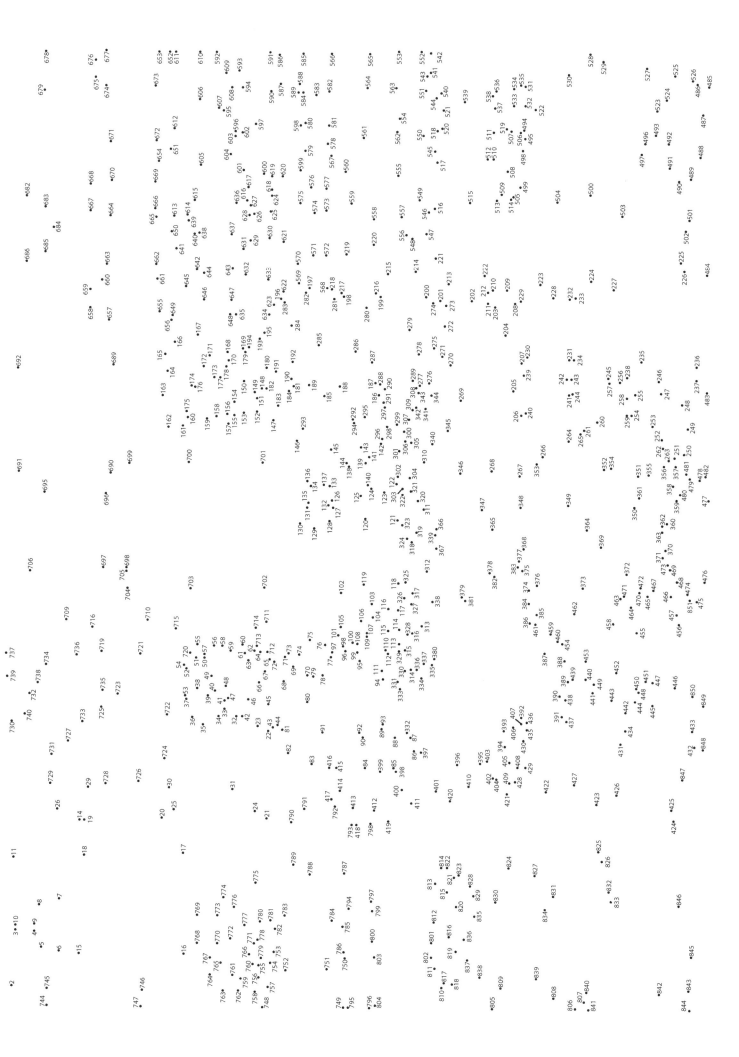

Cafe Scene 28 (835 dots) - Black

Cafe Scene 29 (723 dots) - Black

Cafe Scene 30 (828 dots) - Black

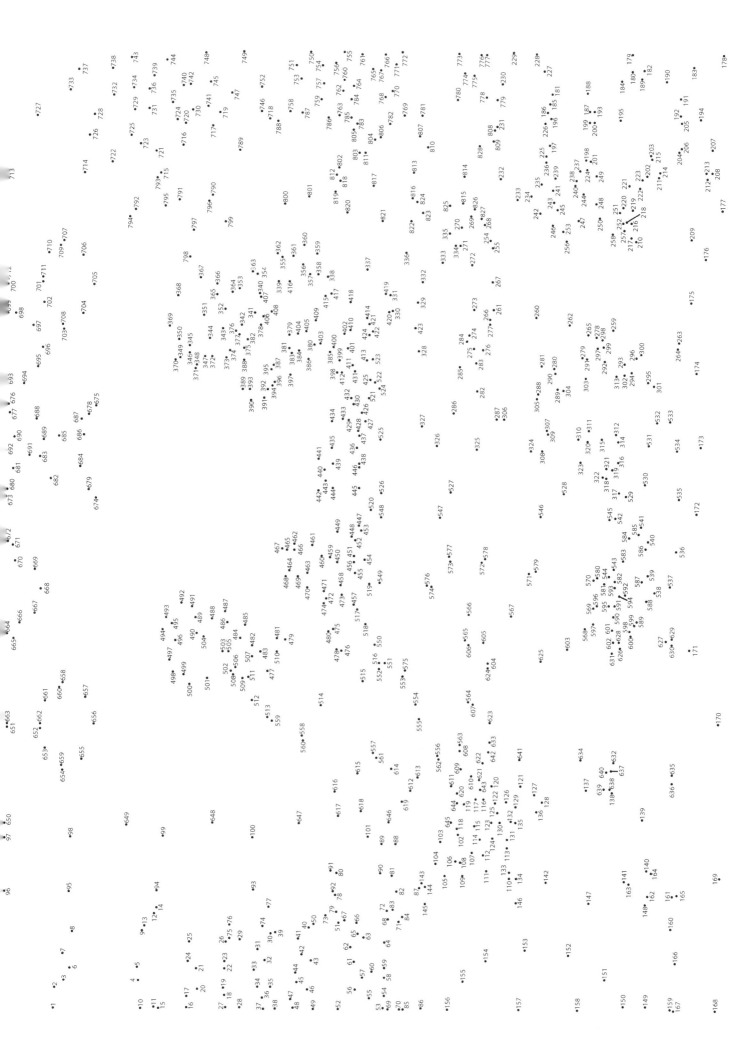

COMPELTED
DOT PAGES PREVIEWS

Completed Dot to Dot Pages Previews

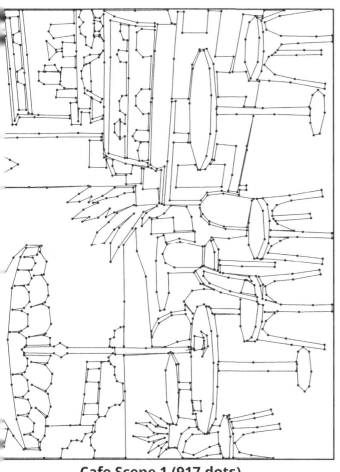

Cafe Scene 1 (917 dots) -

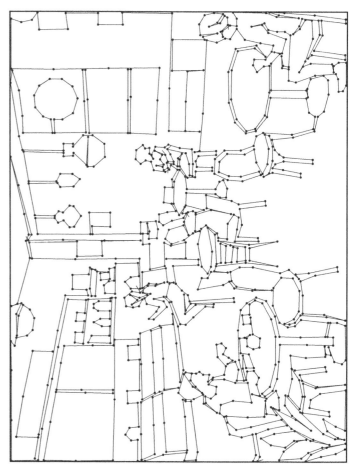

Cafe Scene 2 (938 dots) -

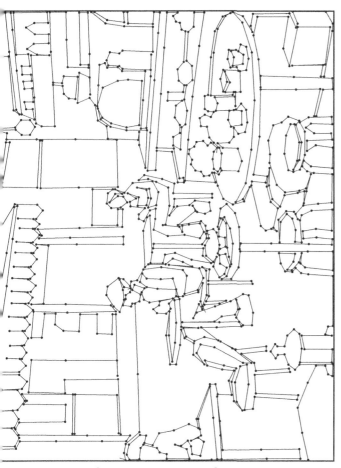

Cafe Scene 3 (1001 dots) -

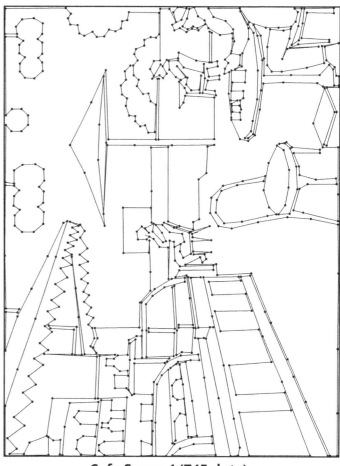

Cafe Scene 4 (745 dots) -

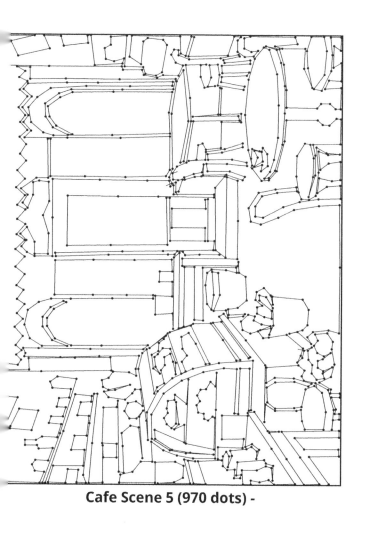

Cafe Scene 5 (970 dots) -

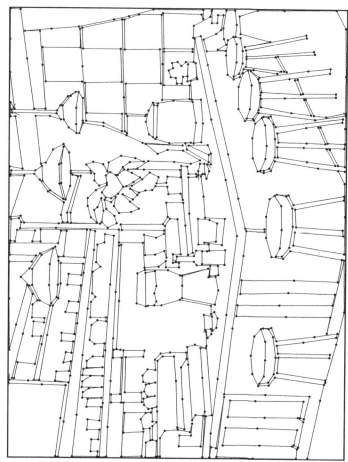

Cafe Scene 6 (903 dots) -

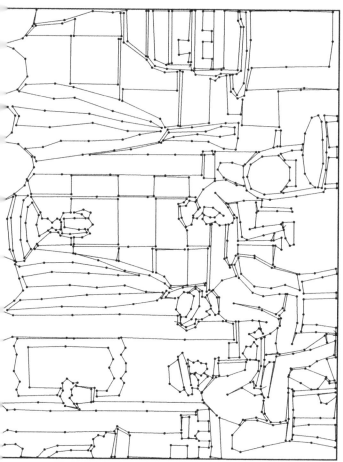

Cafe Scene 7 (900 dots) -

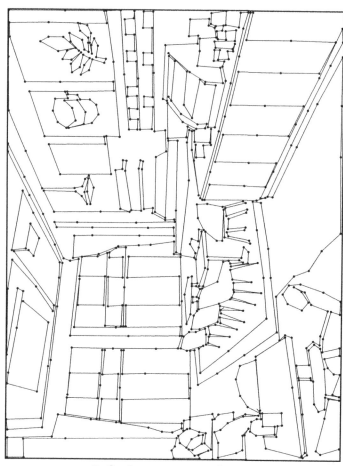

Cafe Scene 8 (705 dots) -

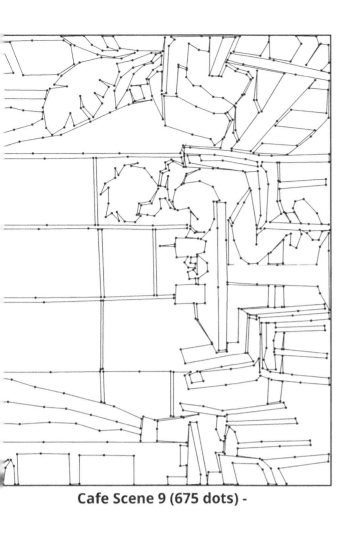

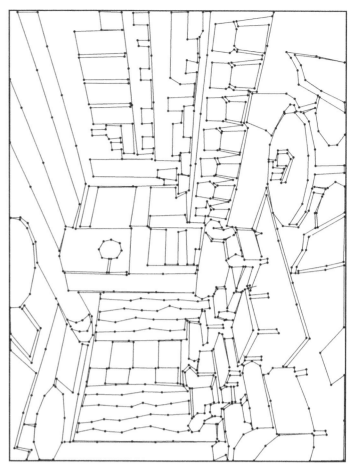

Cafe Scene 9 (675 dots) -

Cafe Scene 10 (779 dots) -

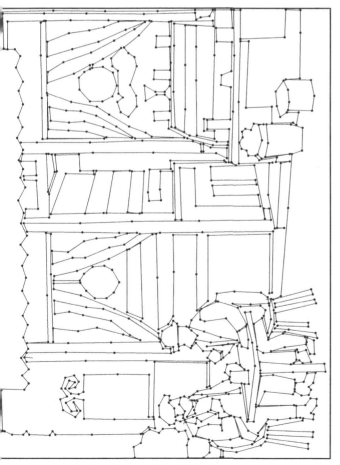

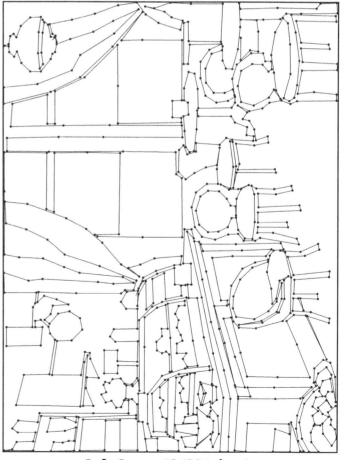

Cafe Scene 11 (805 dots) -

Cafe Scene 12 (804 dots) -

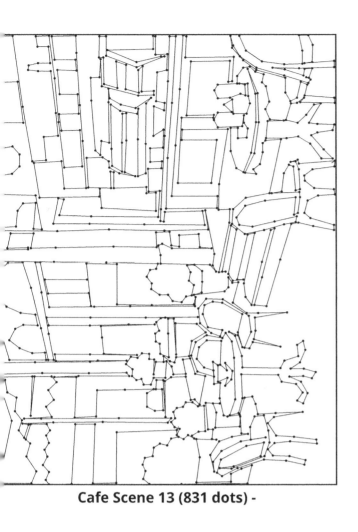

Cafe Scene 13 (831 dots) -

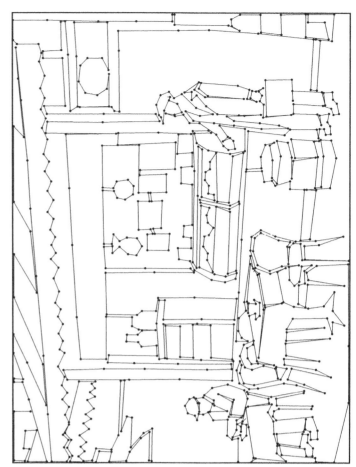

Cafe Scene 14 (772 dots) -

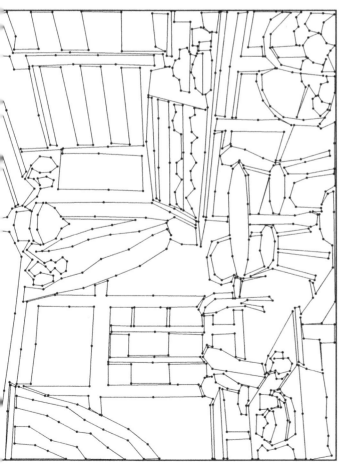

Cafe Scene 15 (784 dots) -

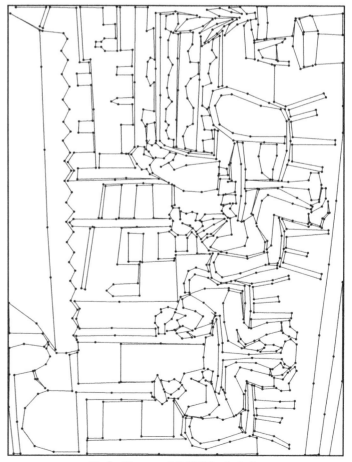

Cafe Scene 16 (920 dots) -

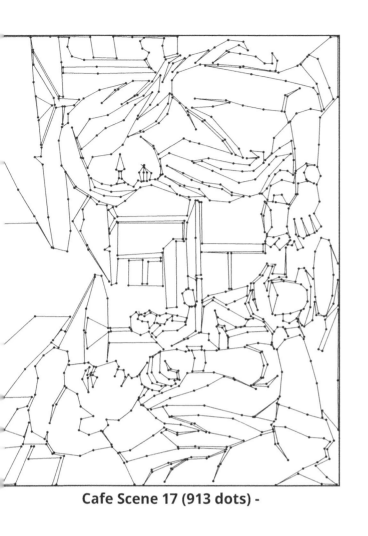

Cafe Scene 17 (913 dots) -

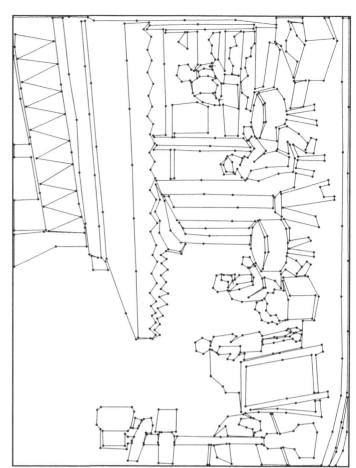

Cafe Scene 18 (718 dots) -

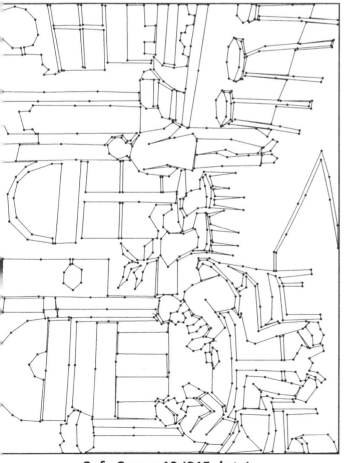

Cafe Scene 19 (815 dots) -

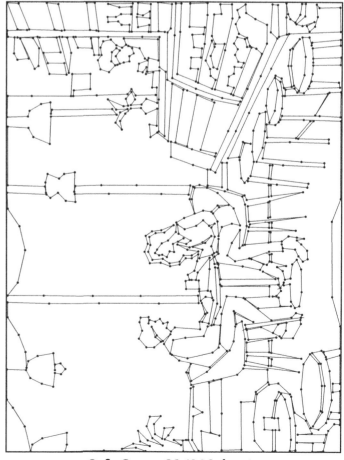

Cafe Scene 20 (916 dots) -

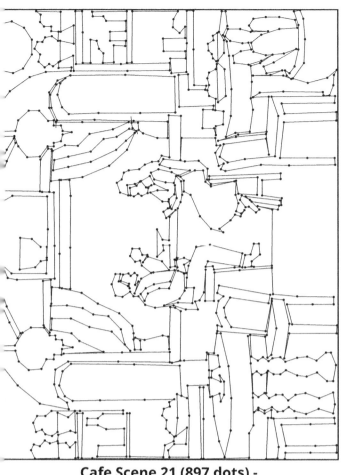

Cafe Scene 21 (897 dots) -

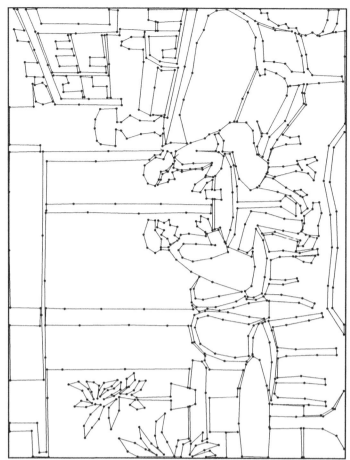

Cafe Scene 22 (796 dots) -

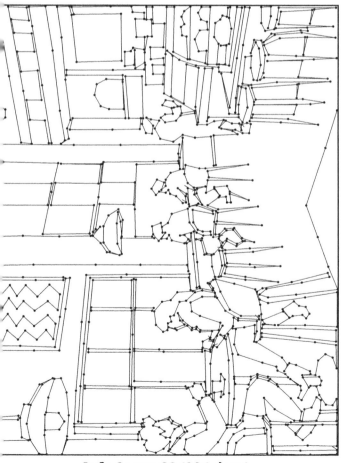

Cafe Scene 23 (994 dots) -

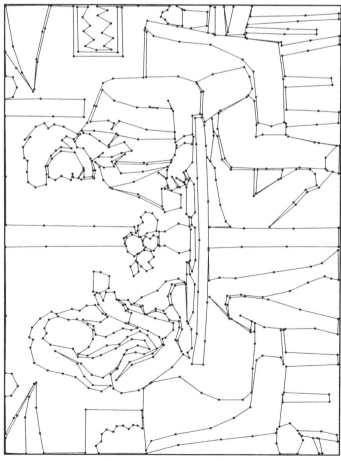

Cafe Scene 24 (704 dots) -

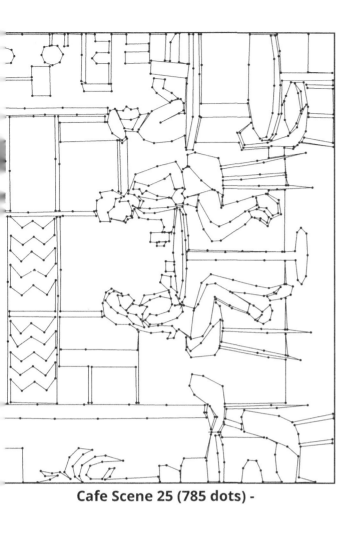

Cafe Scene 25 (785 dots) -

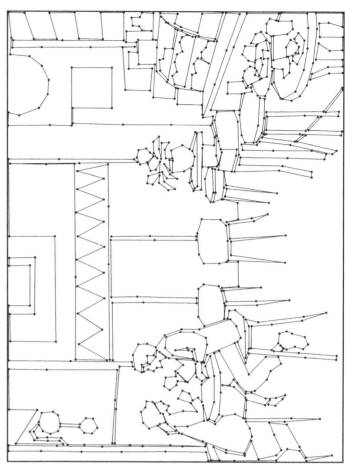

Cafe Scene 26 (753 dots) -

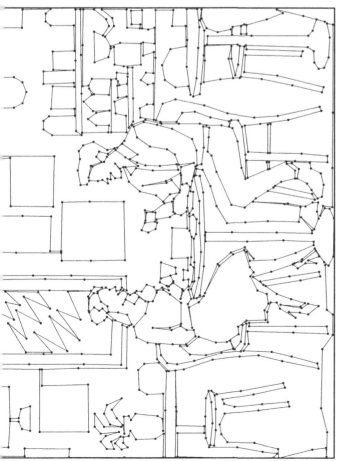

Cafe Scene 27 (851 dots) -

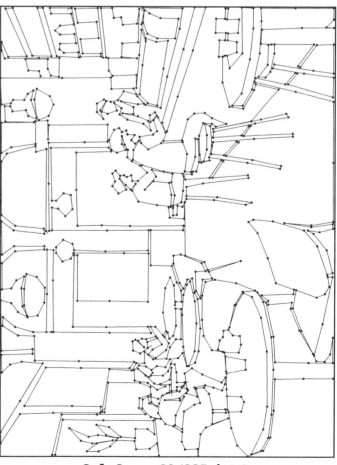

Cafe Scene 28 (835 dots) -

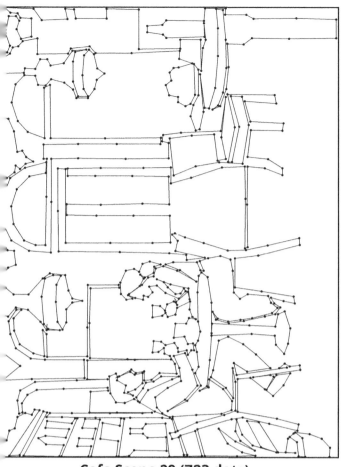

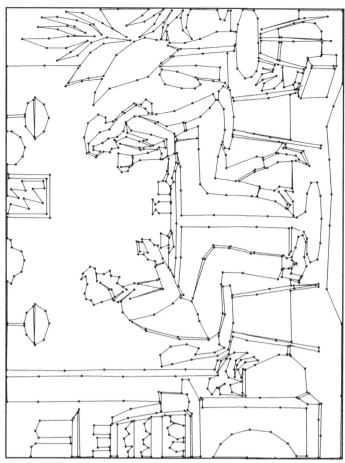

Cafe Scene 29 (723 dots) -   **Cafe Scene 30 (828 dots) -**

Made in the USA
Middletown, DE
08 September 2024

60564984R00046